Parrotfish and Sunken Ships

For Sydney

Parrotfish and Sunken Ships

Exploring a Tropical Reef

Jim Arnosky

Collins

An Imprint of HarperCollinsPublishers

INTRODUCTION

THE ONLY LIVING CORAL REEF in U.S. waters is off the southeastern coast of Florida. This spectacular natural treasure stretches for hundreds of miles along the coastline of the long string of islands known as the Florida Keys. Deanna and I took our boat *Crayfish* to the sun-drenched waters there. At Matecumbe Key we were able to study the entire reef structure—from the shallow reef flats only a few hundred feet from the beach to the reef crest five miles offshore. It was an experience we will cherish forever. Not only did we see the reef and its inhabitants up close, but we also learned a little about ancient shipwrecks and their sunken treasure.

Aye, matey! There's treasure to be found! So come with us aboard our salty little boat and explore the different underwater environs that make up a tropical reef. We'll show you all there is to see, from parrotfish to sunken ships.

The green iguanas
are wild offspring
of released pets.

Night herons are
native to the Keys.

tHERE ARE SIX features that make up a tropical reef. The reef flats is the portion closest to the shore. Just beyond the flats, where the bottom slopes and deepens, clusters of coral dot the ocean floor. These are called patch reefs. Beyond the patch reefs is a trough, or channel of deeper water. After the channel, the bottom gradually climbs and the back reef begins. The back reef gently slopes upward to become the reef crest. After the crest, there is a front slope that drops steeply to the depths of the open sea.

Crayfish was docked in Matecumbe Key, in the protected waters of a quiet little canal. To get to the reef, we had to follow the canal out to an inlet that led us to the ocean. Each morning as we slowly made our way through the canal, we were watched from the trees by green iguanas and sleepy-eyed night herons.

Parts of a Tropical Reef

Reef flats   Patch reefs   Channel   Back Reef   Reef crest   Front slope

Even at high tide, the water on the flats is only shin deep near shore. It's knee deep one hundred feet out, and no more than four feet deep five hundred feet out.

In the crystal clear, light-saturated water of the flats, fish and other aquatic creatures appear so suddenly, they seem to materialize before your eyes.

Barracuda

Barrel sponge

Jack crevalle

Moon jellyfish

Loggerhead sea turtle

Stingray

Sergeant major

Puffer

Trunkfish

Lizardfish

Needlefish

Nurse shark

There are three ways you can search for marine life in the shallow water of the reef flats. You can wade. You can snorkel. Or you can drift slowly in a boat. Deanna and I enjoy doing all three. Whichever method of exploring you choose, the longer you look, the more you see.

On the Matecumbe flats, we have seen fish of all shapes and sizes. Curious puffers, needlefish, and box-shaped trunkfish have followed our boat. While flyfishing, I caught a strange little fish that looked more reptile than fish. It was a lizardfish!

Nurse sharks hardly ever venture from the area where they were born. Nurse sharks are everywhere on the flats, but mostly you will see them foraging for crabs in the sea grass. Sea grass provides shelter and food for crabs, mollusks, and fish.

Sea grass blades are encrusted with nutrient-rich organisms.

A living conch's shell is coated with algae.
An empty conch shell is clean and shiny.

Florida fighting conch

The reef flats are where we find conchs (pronounced CONKS). The largest conchs are the Florida fighting conchs and the queen conchs.

One day Deanna came upon a nudibranch (pronounced NOODIBRANK) swimming near the surface. Nudibranchs are mollusks very similar to conchs, but they live without the protection of a shell.

Hermit crabs use empty mollusk shells for protection. They crawl around carrying the borrowed shells on their backs. Most hermit crabs are small. Deanna and I once found a hermit crab that was gigantic living inside a large queen conch shell! It took a whole page in my journal to sketch it life-sized.

Bonefish are called the "ghosts of the flats" because their silver bodies reflect both the under surface of the water and the sandy sea floor, at times making them almost invisible.

Queen conch

Nudibranch

Hermit crab

Bonefish

Mullet

Mullet are similar in color and shape to bonefish.

Just beyond the flats, *Crayfish*'s depth sounder measured eight, ten, and then twelve feet of water beneath us. A light wind was rippling the surface, and through the ripples we saw large dark shapes on the sea floor. At first I thought they were rocks and I motored over them carefully. Hitting a large high rock can ruin a boat's propeller.

When the wind died down, the water calmed, and we could see all the way to the bottom. What I thought were rocks were actually chunks of old coral. Each small outcropping of old coral was a separate patch reef with an abundance of living coral and sponges growing on it and whole schools of fish swimming around it.

Sea rod

Rock beauty

Redband parrotfish

Tube sponge

Because of all the algae growing on the old coral, the patch reefs were dark and mysterious looking. There were lots of crevices for small fish to hide in. The larger crevices made ideal lairs for moray eels. Blacktip sharks and cobia patrolled the food-rich patch reefs like shoppers in a market.

Against the dark algae that covered the coral, bright-colored tropical fish looked even brighter.

Blacktip shark

Cobia

Spadefish

Loggerhead sponge

Green moray

Red fire sponge

Of all the tropical fish, our favorites are the parrotfish. Whenever Deanna and I are snorkeling over coral, we are always nudging each other to point out these beautiful creatures. Parrotfish are as colorful as birds and have sharp parrotlike beaks that are strong enough to cut stone. While eating the algae that grow on coral and underwater rocks, parrotfish crunch up the coral or rock surface into a fine powdery sand. This sand eventually washes ashore.

There are many different kinds of parrotfish. Here is just a sampling, with some snappers and a grouper in the scene to show the difference between typical fish mouths and the unusual beaklike mouth of parrotfish.

Stoplight parrotfish

Blue parrotfish

Queen parrotfish

Midnight parrotfish

The rainbow parrotfish is one of the largest parrotfish.

Rainbow parrotfish

It is believed that parrotfish account for most of the sand found on tropical beaches.

Striped parrotfish

Yellowtail snapper

Grouper

Fan coral

We left the patch reefs and headed out into the deeper water of the channel that parallels the Keys. The water was calm, with gently rising and falling swells. All over the surface, undulating with the swells, were floating masses of sargassum weed. The yellow weed islands drifted slowly by.

Sometimes the fishing is good around sargassum weed. So I stopped and fished awhile but had no luck. While we drifted along with the weeds, a pod of bottlenose dolphins swam by. We have often seen dolphins in the channel, using the deep, open water to race north or south to new feeding areas. We've also seen spotted eagle rays, manta rays, and hammerhead sharks. Once I saw a huge manatee migrating southward. I painted a manatee in this scene so you can see how big a fully grown manatee is compared to our nineteen-foot boat.

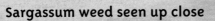

Sargassum weed seen up close

Fish are attracted to floating sargassum weed to feed on the smaller marine animals that hide in the tangle of stems and leaves.

A little way north in the channel, in eighteen feet of water, we came upon a large elongated pile of boulders all by itself on the sandy bottom. These were rocks—all small and round in shape—the remains of an ancient shipwreck! Early ship-builders used boulders as ballast to keep a ship from becoming top-heavy when the sails were hoisted. Only carefully chosen egg-shaped river rocks with no sharp edges would not dig or cut into the ship's wooden hull.

In the 1700s whole armadas of Spanish ships carrying gold and silver from the New World sailed past the Florida Keys on their way home to Spain. In 1733 a hurricane drove an entire fleet of treasure-laden ships onto the jagged reef. After hundreds of years on the sandy bottom, the ships' timbers rotted away. Only iron anchors, cannon, treasure, and the ballast stones remained. In the 1970s treasure hunters began locating the old ballast piles. The pencil drawing shows what this wreck site might have looked like before the treasure hunters picked it clean.

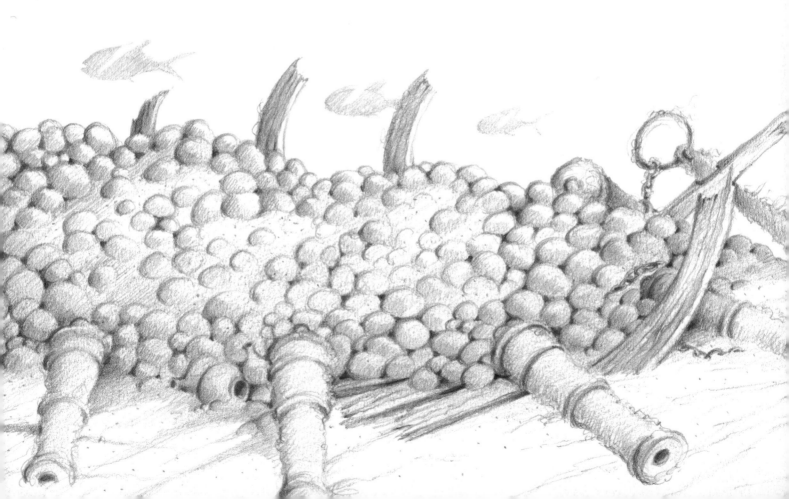

A Spanish galleon was a large ship capable of carrying tons of gold and silver, along with a battery of heavy cannon. But sheer size and weaponry could not insure that a ship's precious cargo would reach its destination. Storms took their toll of ships. And treasure-laden galleons were regularly ambushed by pirates hiding in the shallow bays of the Florida Keys.

Treasure hunters diving down to the wrecks have recovered millions of dollars' worth of gold and silver coins and bars, jewelry, and gemstones. They've also found antique glass bottles, pottery, daggers, and swords.

The ballast piles of ancient shipwrecks have become artificial reefs
providing homes and hiding places
to numerous marine species. In
modern times, some decom-
missioned ships have been
sunk purposely to create
marine habitat.

There are ancient shipwrecks yet to be discovered and long-lost treasure to be found. But until the treasure hunters or Deanna and I or you find them, they will lie undisturbed on the bottom in places known only to the creatures of the sea.

Atlantic spadefish

Bluehead

Spiny sea urchins

Staghorn coral

Sea star

Grunt

Deanna and I began our day in the canal slowly making our way to the ocean. We drifted over the reef flats and cruised a mile offshore to the patch reefs. Then, heading north in the deep channel, we came across the remains of a Spanish galleon.

Hogfish

Houndfish

Filefish

Beyond the channel, about four miles offshore, the bottom climbed and the water gradually became shallower and shallower. This was the back reef. The water was crystal clear. We could see underwater sponges and corals covering the sea floor almost all the way to the reef crest. Here the crest is called Alligator Reef after the 1822 wreck of the naval schooner USS *Alligator*. Alligator Reef Lighthouse now warns mariners of the dangerous reef lurking beneath the surface.

Flying fish

Trumpetfish

Tiger shark

Amberjack

Many of the fish species that live in the back reef also inhabit the reef crest, the reef slope, and the deep water of the open ocean.

The reef crest, with its richly varied coral clusters, is the crowning glory of the entire reef system. Look at this scene with your hands cupped around your eyes as though you are looking through a diving mask. Then look up the names of all the species of fish and coral you can remember seeing. This is the way Deanna and I learn everything—first through our own experiences and then from books. It will take you awhile to recall and identify the fish. Look at the scene as often as you need to, to refresh your memory.

Corals are easy to learn to identify. If it looks like a mountain, it's a mountain coral. If it looks like a branch, it's a branch coral. If it looks like a deer antler, it's a staghorn coral. Fan shaped equals fan coral. Tube shaped equals tube coral. If it resembles flowers, it's a flower coral. If it has little stars all over it, it's a star coral. And if it looks exactly like a giant brain, you guessed it!

Hint: In this scene there are five butterfly fish, two parrotfish, one damselfish, one grouper, one drum, one reef crab, one spiny lobster, one cardinalfish, two morays, one surgeonfish, and one starfish.

We came back from the reef with the memory of all we had seen swimming in our brains. Passing the jetty at the inlet that led to our canal, Deanna photographed a gallery of waterbirds perched on the rocks. It was a perfect way to end the day.

With *Crayfish*'s engine purring, the birds squawking, and Deanna happily snapping picture after picture, I steered through the narrow waterway to our dock. We were explorers, home from the sea.

Using a map of the Florida Keys, you can pinpoint the places explored in this book. Here are the exact locations measured in the degrees and minutes of latitude and longitude. The top number is latitude. The bottom number is longitude.

You will see that, going out and coming back, Deanna and I covered approximately fifteen miles of water. That's only a drop in an ocean of wonders.

THE REEF FLATS } 24° 51'
                 80° 44'

THE PATCH REEFS } 24° 50.2'
                  80° 44.5'

SPANISH GALLEON } 24° 51.3'
  ballast pile   80° 40.5'

THE BACK REEF } 24° 51.5'
                80° 37'

THE REEF CREST } 24° 51'
                 80° 37.2'

THE FRONT SLOPE } 24° 50.2'
                  80° 37'

J.A.

Collins is an imprint of HarperCollins Publishers.

Parrotfish and Sunken Ships
Copyright © 2007 by Jim Arnosky

Manufactured in China.

Library of Congress Cataloging-in-Publication Data is available.
ISBN-10: 0-688-17123-0 (trade bdg.) — ISBN-13: 978-0-688-17123-0 (trade bdg.)
ISBN-10: 0-688-17124-9 (lib. bdg.) — ISBN-13: 978-0-688-17124-7 (lib. bdg.)

Typography by Stephanie Bart-Horvath
1 2 3 4 5 6 7 8 9 10
❖
First Edition